WOVEN LANDSCAPES

AVALANCHE /^\ BOOKS

Published in Great Britain by Avalanche Books, England 2016

Printed by SRP, England

The moral rights of the authors have been asserted.

British Library Cataolguing in Publication Data. A catalogue
record for this book is available from the British Library.

ISBN: 978 1 874392 80 4

Supported using public funding by

ARTS COUNCIL
ENGLAND

LOTTERY FUNDED

Contents

Roselle Angwin

Wendy French

Katrina Porteous

Anne Caldwell

Kaye Lee

Katherine Gallagher

Roselle Angwin

APPLE TREE

Wassail night has passed and winter's
blue flames have retreated for now.
In the orchard, a thrush stabs the last
soft apple, and another calls from the tallest
tree. If you were to come by here, come
and stand by me here, I would hold
your palm to the trunk, tell you how to open
the eyes and ears of your hand so you
could feel how again the xylem and phloem
are waking, making their long slow
streaming journey between earth and star,
if you were to come here, to come by here again.

water and minerals

9

ELECTION

A morning yellow as butter.
In the privet hedge, the sparrows
taste it. History
only takes one route: gestures
at what might have been had we not
messed up.
   The high mass
of clouds spell rain - but not today.

This inbreath.
   In an alternative history
the blossom on the old apple tree
could be a quiet declaration of hope
of the end of the white noise
we visit on the universe.

What matters: whether, and how much,
we care.

SUN

How would it be to be
simply *here,* like that giving
the sunlight does so freely
on the skin of the waterfall pool
on the dragonfly's wings?

Last night, after the meal
and the laughter on the summer
terrace, we walked back
looking into star-time
and not talking

And then in the early hours
the dream visits again:
my father not dead but dying
and again a harrowing, an initiation
by fire and a reminder of

how hard it is to live
simply, like sunlight,
when you're merely
human and mortal, not an
elemental necessity.

THEN TO LET GO

In the night the small rain
    visits the river with its mouths

~

how many years have I thought of you
day upon day carried further
yet your ever-presence

~

the way summer will take us
in our chests as far as
the deepest snows of winter
and then leave us there

~

The quiet house

hammock swinging gently
as if someone's just left

in the early light
    to walk into the hills
        and perhaps keep walking

Yesterday in a moment
	in the Buddha Garden
with Sarah, a sparrowhawk
	zipped through at eye-height
like steely lightning, like inspiration
	- swift laceration at the sternum
wishbone pulled apart. suddenly pinning me
to one moment
almost a grace descending in the wake
	of the predator

~

an early car on the switchback
	of the valley road

how many years has it taken me
to learn not to look down
	to drive into, not around
		this precipitousness

~

one of the gifts now
learning to *inhabit* my life
rather than perch on it −

	to love this transient

vintage wine of me, of us, of it all –
with all that I am –

to drink the deep ruby darkness

then to let go

THE LAST OF THE LIGHT, ISLE OF IONA

The stones hold the memory of the beginning;
waves are the ocean's breath.
A question the colour of silence.

Always the search brings us back -
a longing so keen it's like the wind's
edge; has no words. Voices

come from the island behind the island;
faint as haar on the tongue; your hair
is damp with the blue of them.

One hare leaping. A heartbeat. If on
a spring gloaming you stand near
the *machair,* not far from the Fairy Mound,

you can almost catch the silence
behind the silence; scent of wild
thyme; bells from the silver bough.

Write a love letter to the wind, the rain,
the first and last breaths. Write it in otter track,
in the gannets' dive. Tell me, where does

the ringed plover hide? And who can still tell
of the *oran mor,* the slow deep earth song
from the brimming wells of the Otherworld?

THREE SPELLS OF WATER

i
On the horizon
clouds are the distillate
of the city's years
upcycled, reseeding
the dream of the earth.

Our hearts are dry.
Let there be water.

ii
Later we walked where once the land
was flooded, made an inland sea –
is a moat a keeping-in
or a keeping-out?

'Bridge' spells a different message –
is a welcome,
an act of kindness.

iii
The lost wells of the city
are the memory-keepers,

The silver bowl beside this lady-well
is a catchment for cloud,
for sky, for silence;
for what we have forgotten.

PORPOISE, SANDEELS BAY

How the darkness must have thrashed
with your refusal of this alien element

its gravity, its tug where you couldn't be fluid
and how long this must have gone on

with your whistles and hums and none
of your kind coming, nor the tide

while we inland slept easy under our duvets
just short of the sea, its roars and murmers

– though below, nearer bedrock, in our dreams
darkness scratched a jagged line across our deeps.

HOME

From the window my father
points at the Spanish bluebells
that someone else is tending
and tells me he dug them up
from lanes near a beach not far away
and not long ago
yes I say and yes
I remember – though I know
that in his mind he is back
in the old walled garden
with my dark-haired smiling mother
sixty miles and forty years away

though I know that in his mind
he is young and she is not yet dead

18

FOR WHAT REMAINS UNSPOKEN

Last night there were too many
stars for the sky to hold without dropping

the older ones sang
like owls.

This morning you notice new blossom
mauve and jubilant
in the January hebe.

In the damp courtyard
the tabby cat strolls towards two fat magpies
puffed with cold
who eye her and don't move.

This is how it will happen eventually –
perhaps rainclouds, perhaps evening –

perhaps you hold still, let
the starlight fall down on your face
let the darkness come.

WHEEL

The winds travelling
in their great pereginations –
the migrations of spring,
updraught of summer,
autumn calling it all back,
winter's frosty unbirthings.

How is it we ever fear we're lost,
caught up in this perennial trawlnet
slipstreaming the seasons
through a million trillion galaxies? –
This finding, this holding,
This once-and-for-all belonging.

Wendy French

SAPPHO

their heart grew cold
they let their wings down
Sappho Fragment 42

Sappho   so I read
dived in blue waters   green
in the deepest depths
but you   feet first into the Thames

Sappho whose book
by your bed
would have looked up   to see
olive trees   small fruits longing

the tug of sea water in the river
Big Ben   time not registered
cold bridge remote
from any Greek island

Sappho gasped   drank in salt water
hands down down
reaching for layers of sand
pale silk clinging

hair piled high   on a painted urn
no rest in murky waters
with Sappho   you're there
in the ache of the water's pace

23

WINTER WEATHERS

because Thor has been at work again
and no one ever answers the telephone
and because the persistent tone of the ring

takes me down the line to where you might be
near the upturned umbrella abandoned
on Pendine Sands or blown to sea

and because you lost umbrella after umbrella
like that blaming the new winds
the in-coming tide always finding an excuse –

because of all these signs or omens of wet sands
ferocious clouds salt water seeping through shoes
the tufts of grass on the cliffs daring to raise their heads

before morning and because when you opened the door
that final time and said, *This is it* and it was it
I have to believe you're riding the amber storm

sailing the over-turned seas in a time I didn't know
and maybe you're still dancing and maybe
somewhere is that scarlet dress

WINTER SCENE

'it is an honour to be here, the great esteemed leader,'
Tom in a letter home from Pyongyang 2016

The words you wear are heavy –
you write of water shortage – the bitter cold,

and how you've moved, enticed by a generator.
These uncensored facts can be read elsewhere.

It is cold here too, snow-flakes this morning
and your step-father wonders how you are

as he dreamt of the unimaginable
that is now your country.

He looks through the window and remembers
the excitement of the first sledge he made

and how you cried when he made you leave the park.
Night falling. All of this carried within.

Winter makes your absence stranger.
While I sleep you are closer than during the day.

In daylight I dare not think of you,
Ice on windows, frost over a lawn. These are enough.

25

THE WORK OF RAIN

Gardens still slide into stormy seas reminiscent
of my father's words as he looked through the window,

The old bench is rollicking on the waves
and the Turner painting crooked on the landing.

Summer or winter, rain flooded the shop on the corner
which sold stacked tins of broken biscuits,

a toothless woman serving treats, ha'penny chews,
on the wall pictures of sailors, sons. Sunk at sea.

Rain turned dusty days and parties to wash-outs,
while teenage years rampaged like floods through
                                                    streets,

with the aftermaths of broken love affairs.
Then the rain in the Elan Valley walking with him,

knowing that the mist was heaven descending,
hugging branches to embrace the cold of the wet.

Now driving rain slashes streets that lead to Pendine
                                                    Sands,
the sun and its helix have disappeared, waves hit the
                                                    shore

foaming with language, the future-perfect poked into
                                        pockets,
I will have taken it home. It's impossible to drown
                                        absence –

waves carry it back, away and back.

UNTITLED/UNNAMED

The willow pattern plates
balance on the welsh dresser
catch the sunlight
from cornfields

the old woman dusts
each plate
even the cracked one
dropped once

on purpose
broken repaired
reminds her
of when her body

craved sun
was beautiful

and how much each day hurt then

THE PROCESSION

What is this dream I hear when horses
don't gallop away? Stay nuzzling each other
as earth is dug, heaved, shovelled to one side.
With the roses' scent my sister returns

as I push my grand-daughter round
West Norwood Cemetery, we walk slowly
follow a West Indian procession –
four traditional cob stallions draw

a carriage with Joseph, cornflowers tell us
his name – and mourners serious as clouds
overhead but I have to draw back
from the crowd as Isabella squeals

with delight at the horses' plumes and shouts,
Move, faster, faster, faster, come on. Move
and then far away from the stallions here
are other horses who drift in and out

of clouds like mist over the field,
these beasts who graze behind the white-washed house
nearing the end of the primrose lane where
once we lived forty odd years ago –

hundreds of miles away –
horses turned out to grass at three pm daily
who if they could see us coming
would jostle to be first at the fence.

AN INCONSEQUENTIAL PHOTOGRAPH

The way the camera's angled makes it hard to see
whether the gin's half full but the tonic's empty
beside the blackened saucepan which holds gnocchi
next to the sausage fry-up.

It's hard to see whether there are cherries left on the
                                          trees; perhaps
we've eaten them as they dropped, dark, almost black,
                                          into our hands –
you're never in the photographs, claiming you're the
                                          only one
who can hold the camera steady.

It's hard to see who's talking but there's laughter as we
                                          remembered
the slowworm that slithered through the stillness when
                                          we arrived
and you threw the blue cloth over the table to make life
                                          respectable
before adding forks, neatly polished glasses.

We're poised like a summer sketch found in an old
                                          notebook
and I think blue cloth, cherries, against a back-drop of
                                          horses
who saunter to the fence in the hope of apples or
                                          recognition
of their part in the frame.

It's hard to know how the photograph popped up on to
                                    my screen
without being called; it's distracted the task in hand and
                                    now hours
have been wasted looking for the sign of a cherry,
                        horses, common nouns
that were important, that stay fixed.

KNIGHT MOVE

How we could all come to love the road,
to want to be travellers, driving the highway,
the sun behind us, following the truck
with the soldiers singing.
If I could play that game of chess again
you'd win because I'd be too slow to make
a move. The sun on its chosen path would pursue
your words, *this is the last time we'll laugh like this.*
                    To be on a road that led
from nowhere to here, turn right at crossroads
into early sunrises, bright kitchens, the cream frozen
on the doorstep milk; if I could do all this I'd learn
how to take your bishop, change your move.
You'd have been the one to join in with whoever was
                             singing.

Katrina Porteous

ELECTROMAGNETISM
Excerpt from 'Field'

If there is a beginning
This is its signature.
Its first scribble.

Not a continuum.
Only the sum
Of countless discrete

Shivers, a meaningless
Cipher that becomes
Gas, dust, and at least

One exquisite accident –
An instrument
To interpret its imprint.

Astonishing that, across
Immense distance,
It should speak,

Cold and articulate
As zigzags of light.
And if an infant

Cannot translate –
Cannot receive
Its message –

Still, it is born
Hard-wired, of the one
Unnegotiable grammar.

GRAVITY

After Miroslav Holub
Excerpt from 'Field'

Here, too, the peaks and valleys,
Planets, moons, stars
Rolling, helpless, in rivers.

Here, too, the circle-dance,
The soundless music
Writing its order in deep space.

A map of all possible relations.
Tendencies towards or away from.
Here, too, the familiar geographies –

Stretching, pushing out
On something pressing back.
The embattled stars'

Eventual collapse.
The madly-spinning catherine-wheel's
Demonic pulse.

Here, too, the roaring falls.
Oblivion. The river
Tearing faster and faster.

FREQUENCIES
Excerpt from 'Sun'

How does the Sun flow?
It secrets
Darker than an ocean's strangeness.

Let the waves tell us.

Each an explorer,
Tasting its own precise

Level; speeded or slowed
By the hazards it endures.

No journey was ever so extreme.

And not one traveller
Returns unchanged. Each time,

It brings back its unique
Report, exact as light.

AURORA

Sometimes in the high latitudes
The whole night
Writhes in its prison.

Green sheets thrash
And twist in an unknown
Wind, wild rivers

Making for elsewhere
In the dark. Particle,
Wave, in ever-changing

Torrents, caged
And volatile, the invisible
Meeting itself in disguise,

Arrives, alight,
To remind Earth of its own
Incalculable strangeness.

MOON
Excerpt from 'Edge'

Too long in the oven, a grey cinder.
A pumice-stone. A lump of clinker.

Snowshine grit, asbestos desert,
Your daylight sky as black as velvet,

Knife-edge salt-ridge building-site,
A cold dead ash-can, emptied out,

White-out stoneyard. Nothing's mirror,
Stripped of sound, leeched of colour.

Fossil footprints. In the distance
The tremor from some random violence.

Scrapyard. Relic. Extinct war-zone,
Blasted. Battered. Uproar frozen

Ever-after, moments smashed
Into grains of powdered glass

Stacked up in their billions,
Fixed in a snapshot's flinty brilliance –

A stillness, exquisitely balanced
On the needle of this silence.

PASSAGE MIGRANTS

It has taken a long time
To reach here – countless

Wing-beats, a hunger
To go, without knowing where.

Each time, the same –
Desolate, the tundra.

Stint, sandpiper, rising.
Deserts to cross. Between,

This precise place:
The Pleistocene shore,

Stitched with worm,
Riveted with barnacle,

Its rank guts a fulcrum;

A feast timed
To the tide's pendulum;

Sea-wracked, its rocks
An archive of climate

Locked up like coal.
There are still places

On Earth so remote
They are without shelter.

Their messengers alight
Here, for a moment,

Before the flood's broom.

SPACE TELESCOPE
Excerpt from 'Edge'

Infant, afloat in austere space,
Plump, dependent body tethered
By your tough umbilicus,
Face a mirror full of darkness;

Exquisite machine, your tinfoil
Wings, your booms' mosquito lightness,
Carrying our human hunger
Into the perpetual silence –

Intercede for us. The mountain
Cocks its ears, the wilderness
Of holy madmen strains to listen
For a song beyond extinction.

INTERTIDAL
Beadnell, 2015

I walked out to the end of the Broad Rock
At low spring tide. A prehistoric
Foreshore, empty pavement, jagged, violent

Brown stone, broken apart under the sky's
Hammer. Strange shrieks. Wild shouts loosed from
                                        somewhere

Very far away – vast, wide, metallic,
Mineral. In every seam and channel,
Slippery, smelling briny with excitement –

Beards, groins, armpits, dripping pelts
The colours of old bronze, dried blood, new grass –

Carrageen, corallina, sea-oak, saw-wrack,
Unpicking the chemistry of air, salt water, sunlight.

Before me, kelp beds, freshly-exposed; then the sea's
                                        glitter –
Green algae, gobbling the red gleam close to the surface.
Red algae, eating the blue gloom in the deep water.

The tawny, the ochre, leathery, rubbery, feathery –
Floating, provisional, shuffling their elements,

As far as light can penetrate, until
There is nothing here but process.

And I have to turn back.

Anne Caldwell

LUNAR ECLIPSE

The Exe froze over
and the music of the city was hushed.

You watched
the male swans bunch together

in a moon-shaped space of open water
and held your son close to your chest.

Upstream, Leda let her coat slip
from her shoulders onto snow.

She walked out
                of her own free will
to meet that quilled rush of air.

You both stared at her footsteps
in the river-ice and drew each other closer.

Above your heads, a wedge of birds
hooted over and over and over.

CRAB APPLE

That summer of 1976: thousands of ladybirds
scrambling all over the privet, flitting from the
honeysuckle to the crab apple tree, landing on our skin
like spotted kisses. Concrete slabs beneath the washing
line, hot as waffles. We squashed the ladybirds and red
spider mites without mercy, our boredom treacle-thick
punctuated by the rhythmic bounce of a tennis ball
against a wall. There were endless evenings of roller
skating up and down the same street. Standing next to a
telephone box that smelt of rotten fruit trying to ring
some boy without being overheard. Without our dad, our
family house was eider-downed with grief.

BLUE MONDAY

The moon didn't rise tonight. The city's reach pulled us,
the southern sun burned without diminishing. There was
poetry on the radio as blue Monday drifted into Tuesday,
Wednesday. When you caught the clock with
outstretched hands I took my sharpened pencil as a
lover. Good wood. I have now revised a poem to make it
more specific. I recycled, signed petitions, and
remembered when we were pressed together in the busy
vaporetto. Your orange silk shirt wet beneath your
armpits.

SALFORD (1)

The puma padded up Fitzwilliam St, her pelt gleaming,
soaked by days of rain. Salford's gutters were full to the
brim. She dragged her choke-chain through the parking
lots and cobbled back to backs, shied from light spilling
out of Bargain Booze, nosed the chip wrappers and
polystyrene trays. All the while the drizzle came down.
Her eyes reflected sodium glare, taxi hub caps, winking
tower blocks and a Lidl sign. No one noticed her slide
on her belly under galvanized gates to sniff the man's
Harley with its chrome curves, fumes and engine ticking
from a wet commute. The stitched seat was sleek and
beautiful like this cat that searched for a place to sleep.

SALFORD (2)

Her eyes narrowed as he left his door ajar. He stood in
the yard in his rain-soaked leathers, paused for beer and
a smoke. She slipped inside, her gritty paws warmed by
carpet-pile, by the quiet of the house with its fine sight-
lines. Later, he straightened a print; sensed the shadow
of something darker than himself. The house smelt of
freshly coffee, gallery paint. The kitchen hummed as he
slept upstairs. She toppled a carton from the kitchen
worktop, lapping it with her rough tongue as milk
dribbled and pooled on the tiled floor. The photographer
shivered in his sleep, dreaming of a route across the
Dakota plains. She brushed past the cacti on the
windowsill, her flank bristling with filaments. She
cleared his stairs with two jumps, curled at the foot of
his bed, smelt the warmth of his motorway-skin. He
woke to find the puma draped across his shoulders, his
collar-bone scratched. As she licked the salt from his
clavicle, he lay quite still. Listened to her tuned-up,
engine purr.

NIDDERDALE

Alice made a nest of coats in the caravan she borrowed
from a friend. She was off grid. It rained all night,
Nidderdale rain, heavy and persistent, drumming on the
metal roof of her box-shaped room, with the sound of
the river like a bass note in the music of water. Her
father would have remarked, it's raining stair rods, lass
or raining cats and dogs. She thought of Escher's
stairways leading nowhere, the Bourgeois print of a
woman cradling an angry baby at the bottom of a flight
of steps. At night she dreamt of stray terriers falling
from the sky. Would she be furred-in, rather than
snowed in? Limp, sodden bodies piled up against the
cinder blocks of the caravan? Waking to sunshine was a
relief. She parted the yellow beaded curtain and looked
up to the grit-stone moors, birch trees shimmering like
unspoken words…

ABERDEEN ART GALLERY

'*To help us ensure the comfort and safety of all the
visitors to the gallery please do not let children play
with the water in the fountain. Thank you.*'

Fiona and I were folded into a bed
with a pot hot water bottle under a quilt
that remained damp even at the height of June.

There were *butteries* for breakfast. We scrubbed
the bird bath in a garden of gnarled trees,
and floribunda roses past their best.

Later, we strolled along Rosemount Viaduct
to the gallery to stare at carcasses
by Francis Bacon. I sniggered until reprimanded,

felt the chill of granite pillars against my cheek,
then hop-scotched across a chequered floor
as red paint dripped down the canvases.

At midnight, Gran's stairwell clock began to strike.
Lumps of butchered meat and howls
of conscripts from the war filled the bedroom

as I felt for my sister's spine.
I pressed my feet against hers as the sun rose
and traffic roared along Anderson Drive.

LADDER

You text me a pen n' ink sketch
of a ladder that hovers over

> the world's number-crunching
> madness

and these ways we've found
to live our lives: coaches,
buses, cars, trains:

You're in transit from South
to North,
in commuting
back and forth across
the Penines.

And your ladder is a
floating
smile –

> curved around us
> in my stone room.

And now and now?
We have these delicate,
hand-drawn rungs to each other.

Kaye Lee

REBIRTH

Like an oyster shell turned over,
an oil slick caught by sun or an opal sky
painted on a sludge-pond,
all things, viewed closely
give back their primitive perfection -
they cry out with the jewelled voice of a beetle,
dance to the beat of ripples from a twig
dropped in a puddle -
and when we think we've escaped,
flown far from our beginnings,
their voices call us back, lay before us
the land we thought was dead.

STITCHING TWILIGHT
im PDG
after Paul Klee Twilight Flowers

This could be a new embroidery,
one you've made from a grandson's drawing –

see the bird, its beak open
to drink in the last of the daylight

while a scarlet tulip, believer in spring,
leaps over a bonsai wattle tree

stooped beside your fat-as-a-donut cat
who plays ball with the end-of-day sun,

and the giraffe is surely the one from Dubbo Zoo
where we ate cold pasties: it was after Heidi's wedding,

remember, a pause on our three day journey home
when every hill was purple from Paterson's curse.

But it's only a postcard that lies
on the cold tiles by our London door

and though the reds and greens, orange and blue
zing with the heat of your Wimmera home

and the bird seems to be a kookaburra
passing on his favourite joke

when I turn the card over it's an owl
that spells out your name -

you couldn't have sent this card.

SCRAPS OF MIRO BLUE

This spread of blue is the Pacific
lapping Dunk Island.
Dive into it and the blue mutates,
brings shimmers of coral,
parrot fish, clams
closer than fingertips.

Now it's a blue dome – an outback sky
over the red slash of Uluru;
for the diving eagle it's transparency
above a skittering blue-tongue lizard.
Later, night wraps the dome
in rich dark velvet.

And here are the Blue Mountains –
the blue, scientists say, is light
refracted through eucalyptus fumes
but we see a bunyip's shadow
until lightning ignites, creates
a graveyard of black monuments.

It was not by mistake the Old Masters
made heaven blue, a colour
never still, and used it
to clothe the Mother of God,
but how did they, and how
did Miro, hold it steady
as they fixed it to canvas?

BUILDING WITH SAND

In the beginning we didn't want sandcastles –
the sea was for swimming in, the sand
for barefoot running, or for lying on until
our hair and skin crackled dry with salt –

but when we saw those other families
building castles with crooked walls,
towers buckling under faded flags,
we decided we could do better

So, with bucket after bucket of damp sand
we constructed a castle: broad ramparts,
solid walls, sand packed hard as concrete –
not even a tsunami would knock it down.

Inside we made rooms, dragged in rocks
for tables and chairs, reeds to sleep on
and seaweed for curtains and blankets.
It was large enough for all of us

along with our yet-to-be-met husbands,
unborn children and grandchildren, friends,
relatives. We offered advice to our neigbours
as their castles fell each day to the tides.

The crabs surprised us - we didn't expect them
to scrape and burrow in the foundations, collapse
the walls, bury us in mountains of cold sand.
I dig all day, hope to find other survivors.

FOR ELSIE AT 100

I will stroke you with feathers infused
with oil of lavender and attar of roses;
I will loosen your years with beeswax
blended to dews of honey, unroll bandages
of withered flesh and crumbling mind
which keeps you confined and dumb.
Now we can go together, a shuffle
at first, then a walk, faster and faster
until we are running toward the western
mountain beyond the town and there
I will call to the birds of your homeland –
rosellas, kookaburras, galahs – and as
the lyrebird performs his arcane dance
they will lift you up.

Katherine Gallagher

APPENDIX TO A RELATIONSHIP

I
Now we move across countries
        You have already left (in idea)
and we walk with others in a garden
chatting through hours
where our hearts are getting ready

Suddenly a child carries everybody
He's afraid of going too fast in a cart
pulled by an adult
        We'll go slowly
he declares
The guests smile wryly
We smile

II
Our silence gathers
and we know
Keep care in its place
you say
     I muse   wonder
knowing I won't see you again
in years
Here the sky is full-blue
and the ground a coat of daisies

     I don't try to choose the weather
any more.

The turn in somebody's fortune is my eye's
aching for softness with you
among words that touch

Where geography leaps off
                    where the sea
turns silken from a plane-window
where I am a map
without final edges

III
Live with the bones of
private parting

The scene opens out
and I am a wanderer in my own space

          a woman talking to herself
          under her umbrella

You take my arm   How you feel
for me   for us
                    You point out the chestnuts
They are wonderful I agree

What will our words be
in a context of five hundred years

Stone   Bridge   I lean

Things can never be
the same again

A weekend isn't long enough
to chart it all

We are going out of our story
our lesson watched on all sides
sometimes with pity

Our quiet passion
become a silent thing
guarded without comeback

CHOICES

I go to the hedge of our holiday-cottage
to trim branches within easy reach.
I am cutting edgily until two eyes
fix mine. Not a sound passes between us,
but I know we understand each other.
The blackbird on her nest is intent.
Without a second look, I withdraw,
murmuring apologies.

GUIDE AT A PETRARCH EXHIBITION
- Fontaine de Vancluse

He said he'd studied Petrarch for years
and come to know many minstrels in the man
including the famous one who'd seen his *Laure*
leap out of the cloud, the ideal come to life
who stayed in every poem.

But they remained apart, two souls
drawn by their legend. Already married,
she stayed faithful, became Petrarch's muse,
translating his *Canzoniere*.

Their singleness of love sits strangely counterpointed
against lines of different portraits
of the beautiful *Laure*. I'm quite bemused.
The guide smiles at this,
warns me about romantic love.

LOVE-SONGS

I
Blue-mountain-edge in front
and sky coming down rain pounding
       Still the wonder
close to love's delivery
Put your best face on
We could make it thunder
gripping our hands on weather
colder than we'd thought

II
The climate is a twist
of unexpected changes
We will put roads down
nettle our geographies
       Solidly chosen
the house for a lifetime
with high moments knocking
across our questions

III
Beside love's logic
death's a pinpoint
We can put it off
thrust against futures
Now just state priorities
our lives on the roundabout
holding fears to ransom
testing new legends

IV

There where customs ark tradition
beyond today
the archover cathedral of the dream
freeing nature
to landscape our
chosen valley
Across our voices
the celebration lifts

SUBURB

Here the street-lights run in straight lines,
marking the road, the last bulwark against
a wilderness of boxes, successors to the hut,
the tent, the lean-to – set before the elements:
bungalows, the townie's lot, slot, with space for a car
and patio.
         Here within the moving borders,
the houses placed politely, inscrutable
amidst gardens, the odd lawn-mower still chirring
late summer evening before the dew comes down.

VISIT

I
This time, approaching from Orleans,
we didn't see the cathedral stark against

the wheat-lands of *La Beauce*.
Even miles off, we felt its aura, a sacred place

saved through history to witness with messages
of permanence and how we should love one another.

We memorise the faces etched in stone – a tryst
with eternity, coupled to a baby's laugh.

II
In the long dusk, light pierces
the stained-glass –

Chartres welcoming, radiating
candle-glow as a singer enters

asking fabled questions
where each note, each word

is joined to all
that has gone before –

beauty and light shining on
travellers, their pilgrim souls.

BIOGRAPHIES

Roselle Angwin brings a background in creative mythology, Transpersonal Psychology, ecopyschology, Zen and the bardic arts to all her work. Poetry collections include *Bardo* (Shearsman Press) *Looking for Icarus* (IDP) *River Suite* and *All the Missing Names of Love* (IDP)

Wendy French's latest collection of poems, *Thinks Itself A Hawk*, was published by Hippocrates press 2016, Her collaboration with Jane Kirwan resulted in the book *Born in the NHS*, Hippocrates press (2013). She won the Hippocrates Poetry and Medicine prize for the NHS section in 2010.

Katrina Porteous writes about nature and people in Northumberland where she lives. She has written three science-based pieces for Newcastle's Life planetarium with computer composer Peter Zinovieff. Excerpts appear here. Edge was a Poetry Please Special on BBC Radio 4. Katrina's most recent collection is *Two Countries* (Bloodaxe, 2014)

Anne Caldwell is based in Hebden Bridge, West Yorkshire.. Her latest collection is *Painting the Spiral Staircase*, Cinnamon Press, April 2016. Several of her prose pieces emerged from a collaborative project with the International Poetry Studies Institute based at the University of Canberra.

Kaye Lee is a London based Australian poet who has been widely published in poetry magazines and anthologies. Her poems reflect the colour and vibrancy of her native Australia. *'Rebirth' was first published in ARTEMISpoetry.*

Katherine Gallagher is a widely-published Australian-born poet resident in London. She has five full-length poetry collections, most recently *Carnival Edge; New and Selected Poems* (Arc Publications 2010) Her collection, *Acres of Light* will be published by Arc in October 2016. Katherine's poems have been widely translated.